Sherwood Forest

IN OLD PHOTOGRAPHS

Sherwood Forest

IN OLD PHOTOGRAPHS

DAVID OTTEWELL

Nottinghamshire County Council
Leisure Services

ALAN SUTTON PUBLISHING LIMITED

Alan Sutton Publishing Limited
Phoenix Mill · Far Thrupp · Stroud
Gloucestershire

First published 1994
in association with Nottinghamshire County
Council, Leisure Servuces

Copyright © David Ottewell, 1994

British Library Cataloguing in Publication Data.
A catalogue record for this book is available from
the British Library.

ISBN 0 7509 0726 6

Typeset in 9/10 Sabon.
Typesetting and origination by
Alan Sutton Publishing Limited.
Printed in Great Britain by
Hartnolls, Bodmin, Cornwall.

Contents

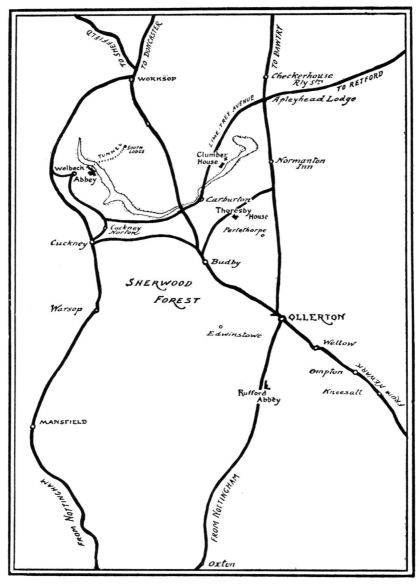

HOP POLE HOTEL, OLLERTON, NOTTS.
CENTRE FOR DUKERIES.   HEADQUARTERS R.A.C.
A. NAISH, PROPRIETOR.

This advertising postcard for the Hop Pole Hotel, Ollerton, was produced by F. Willman of Mansfield for A. Naish, the hotel proprietor, sometime before 1918. It shows the main places in the forest and surrounding area.

Introduction

When William the Conqueror invaded England in 1066 he soon took account of his newly acquired kingdom and decided how it would best serve his purposes. Thus the Forest of Nottingham, covering about 25 per cent of the county, was made one of the royal forests which by the thirteenth century accounted for one third of the land in England. It was used mainly for hunting, with strict forest laws applied to protect the land and its animals.

At this time Sherwood Forest stretched from near Worksop in the north to the River Trent in the south, and from Pleasley in the west to Wellow in the east. It covered an area of land almost 25 miles long and 10 miles wide.

Over the years small portions of the forest were granted for the building of monasteries. Sherwood Forest was a very isolated and inhospitable place, thick with trees and with few paths. A few royal visitors came to hunt but other people, fearing the forest laws, the wild animals and the outlaws, tended to keep away. If people had wanted to settle, the light sandy soil could never have provided good enough crops to support a substantial settlement.

The sixteenth century was the first time of real change, with the dissolution of the monasteries by Henry VIII causing land to fall into the hands of wealthy families. Many trees were felled for shipbuilding and industrial use, and farming became more widespread. The wealthy landowners began enclosing land to make large estates at places like Worksop, Welbeck, Clumber and Thoresby. Many of the estates belonged to dukes, hence the area became known as The Dukeries.

Sherwood Forest became less of a forest as such, with only the Birklands and Bilhagh areas left substantially unaltered. Much of the remainder was under parkland, cultivation or the subject of different degrees of settlement. The advent of the railways in the nineteenth century and the increase in leisure time resulted in an influx of visitors who came to the forest for recreation.

Today the forest survives albeit in a truncated form. Some areas remain inaccessible but one can still appreciate the splendours of Sherwood.

Sherwood Forest to many is synonymous with Robin Hood. Over the years there have been various claims about this character and whether he existed or not. Some even say that he was not a Nottinghamshire man at all but operated in Yorkshire. Whatever the truth behind the legends Robin Hood and his outlaws are still an attractive group to young and old alike and continue to attract interest to Sherwood Forest and the surrounding area.

SECTION ONE
Sherwood Forest

The Major Oak is the most famous tree in the forest, having been, it is claimed, a hiding place for Robin Hood and his men. Until it was fenced off in the 1970s, groups of visitors could stand in its hollowed trunk. There is much contention as to the actual age of the tree.

The Robin Hood connection makes Sherwood Forest the most well-known forest in the world. This statue and the Sherwood Forest bronzes situated on the wall behind were sculpted by James Woodford RA and unveiled outside Nottingham Castle by the Duchess of Portland in July 1952.

Sherwood Forest is said to take its name from 'Shire Wood', i.e. wood of the shire of Nottingham. By the thirteenth century, royal forests covered one third of England and were ruled by strict forest laws.

Sherwood Forest. The term 'forest' does not mean an area of continuous woodland, rather a portion of land subject to forest law. Thus Sherwood has heath, pasture and waste ground as well as trees.

Budby Path. Initially the royal forests were kept exclusively for the use of a wealthy few, and visitors were discouraged until well into Victorian times.

Sherwood Forest. Change began in the sixteenth century, with enclosure, farming and tree felling leading to wider access to and use of the forest.

The Major Oak, situated about half a mile north of Edwinstowe, has a 30 ft circumference and a branch span of 240 ft. It is now the worse for wear and scientists are preparing clones of the tree.

The Major Oak was originally known as the Queen's Oak or Cockpen Tree; its present name comes from Major Hayman Rooke, who catalogued many of the forest trees at the end of the eighteenth century.

The village of Edwinstowe was a staging point for many visitors to Sherwood Forest. The trickle towards the end of the nineteenth century became a flood as improvements were made in transportation and leisure time increased.

Russian hut. After seeing a similar hut on a visit to an exhibition in London in 1874, the 5th Duke of Portland had this hut built of wood in the Russian style without nails. It was a favourite picnic spot for parties from Welbeck and was also used as a shooting box.

The impressive Russian log cabin fell into disrepair during this century and was demolished in the 1950s.

Parliament Oak, situated just outside the Birklands part of the forest, is where Edward I reputedly held a parliament in 1290. In 1915 the sender of this postcard remarked 'Little remains of this Tree'.

Parliament Oak is also claimed to be the site of a meeting between King John and his barons in 1212, when they prepared plans to foil a Welsh revolt.

In 1850 W.H. Thwaites illustrated a book by Pierce Egan entitled *Robin Hood and Little John*. This picture shows Friar Tuck (centre) and other outlaws in the forest.

Robin Hood had a constant battle with the Sheriff of Nottingham, seen here in the royal forest in another illustration by Thwaites.

Thwaites drew Robin Hood and Friar Tuck in combat with staffs – Robin's favourite weapon after the bow and arrow. Another of the famous legends tells how Robin met Little John on a log crossing a stream. The ensuing fight with staffs resulted in Robin being knocked into the water.

The famous death scene has Robin Hood being helped to the window to fire an arrow which would determine his final resting place.

Robin Hood's Larder was where it is said he hung his stolen venison. During this century it suffered fire damage leaving it charred and hollow and open to the elements.

SECTION TWO

Edwinstowe

High Street, Edwinstowe. The newsagents on the left advertises De Reszke cigarettes, while opposite is a sign for Players. Further down on the right is W.S. Lowe's garage and the Kirkstall Café.

High Street. The photographer has moved no more than half a dozen paces from where the previous view was taken, but a whole new perspective is revealed. Notice how most of the advertising signs are not in evidence on this earlier card.

Edwinstowe Church was begun in the late twelfth century, replacing an earlier wooden structure. Legend has it that Robin Hood married Maid Marian here.

The old premises of the Royal Oak seen here in High Street (prior to 1918). It was one of four pubs in the village catering, in 1901, for 986 inhabitants plus visitors. In these earlier, more leisurely days people could stand in the road with little danger of being knocked over.

The Black Swan, the oldest building in Edwinstowe after the church, can be seen on the right of this photograph dating from 1902–4. Further along by the horse and cart is The Jug and Glass, built at the turn of the century. The licensee was Annie Watkin.

A coach outside The Jug and Glass, before the First World War. Coaches on the Dukeries tour stopped in Edwinstowe or Ollerton for their lunch. I wonder how comfortable the ride was.

JUG & GLASS
EDWINSTOWE

An Edwardian view of High Street empty of any form of traffic. To the left can be seen the Co-operative stores built at the end of the nineteenth century with money given by Earl Manvers.

A little further along High Street the photographer has captured a bread van making deliveries.

Cockglode House was built in 1778, an early occupant being Dr George Aldrich. It has latterly been demolished and all traces of the building buried under a colliery spoil tip.

The Hall, Edwinstowe, seen around 1906, is over 250 years old, though it was extended in the nineteenth century. The Countess of Scarbrough and Earl Manvers were previous owners as, in later times, were the Bolsover Colliery Company (from 1929).

STONE LAYING OF NEW SS EDWINSTOWE

TAYLOR PHOTO
WORKSOP

No 1

The stone-laying of the new Sunday school took place on 27 September 1906. The address was by the Revd W.D.L. Slack, and a meat tea, priced 9d, was served. The Sunday school opened in the following February. The photograph was taken by Taylor of nearby Worksop.

Windmills such as this were a common sight around the forest villages. This photograph was taken by R.W. Appleby of Edwinstowe. There were several mills in Edwinstowe including on Mill Lane (which had both a wind and a water mill) and on Mansfield Road.

New Bridge looking towards the station. The bridge took the road over the River Maun. Mill Lane is over the bridge on the right.

Edwinstowe station opened in December 1896. It closed to passengers in September 1964. The Dukeries Hotel, to the left, catered for the railway passengers. The date this photograph was taken is unknown.

The Dukeries Hotel, seen here in the early 1920s, was built in 1897 by Mansfield Brewery. It was badly damaged by fire on 16 February 1929.

The later Dukeries Hotel, extensively rebuilt after the fire but still in a mock-Tudor style.

The upper village and entrance to the forest. Edwinstowe has often been referred to as the 'gateway to the forest'. The house to the right with the steps is Sherwood Villa, built in 1774 and still standing today.

Another view on the way toward the forest; a journey taken by countless tourists over the ages.

The village outskirts and a last opportunity to buy provisions at the little shops, before entering the forest proper.

SECTION THREE
Ollerton

A variety of transport parked outside the Hop Pole Hotel in Ollerton on this postcard by the Nottingham company C. & A.G. Lewis. In the 1920s the publican was John Freeman Jones.

The bridge over the River Maun into Ollerton. On the right can be seen the eighteenth-century Ollerton Watermill. The card was sent by a soldier from Ollerton in August 1916.

The Hop Pole Hotel catered for many coach travellers who often left the Great North Road at Newark and detoured through the picturesque Dukeries before rejoining the highway near Doncaster.

A view from the bridge pictured on the previous page showing Ollerton Hall with the River Maun in the foreground. The postcard was posted in 1922.

Ollerton Hall, seen on an Edwardian postcard. This red brick mansion built by the Markham family replaced an earlier hall built by the same family. It later passed into the hands of Lord Savile. When the nearby pit opened the hall was used as the colliery offices. Today it is in a sadly neglected state.

The road into Ollerton from the Maun Bridge leaving the mill behind to the right and the Hop Pole Hotel to the left. Note the sign for locally made Raleigh bikes.

Further along the road was this rural scene with cattle passing the church and post office.

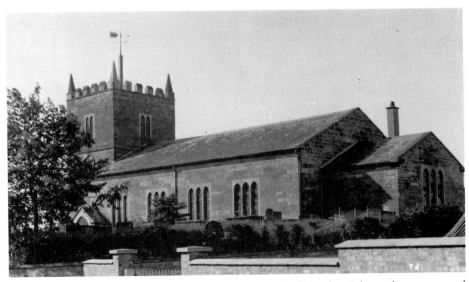

Ollerton Church was dedicated to St Giles. It was built in the eighteenth century and restored in 1860. The postcard writer in 1915 says, 'Ollerton is a small town on G.C.R. (Chesterfield to Lincoln). Train service is poor'.

Looking down the small strip of High Street past St Giles towards Station Road. The card was published by J.S. Viner of Ollerton prior to the First World War.

The White Hart on a postcard posted in 1918. There are a pair of soldiers outside the post office, probably from the large Army camp at nearby Clipstone. Soldiers were encamped on all the Dukeries estates.

The White Hart seen here on an Edwardian advertising postcard when A. Paling was the proprietor. The cart outside was possibly used to transport visitors around the Dukeries. To the left of the inn is the start of the road to Wellow.

On the Wellow road looking down between the church and the White Hart, with a cart just approaching the pub, *c.* 1920. This card was produced by the Doncaster Rotaphoto Co. Ltd.

Another Edwardian view of St Giles, this time looking down Station Road and showing a pair of the many small shops in the village. Again horse-drawn transport predominates.

High Street from the other end of Station Road to that seen on the previous page. Beyond the cart is the Ebenezer Primitive Methodist Chapel built in 1869.

Further along past the chapel, the road winds its way to the village centre on this early 1920s postcard.

Station Road. J.B. Firth in his *Highways & Byways of Nottinghamshire* said of Ollerton, 'The Streets are narrow and the houses common place'. The Doncaster publisher E.L. Scrivens captures this mood perfectly.

Station Road looking the opposite way to the previous card. Notice the horse droppings in the road.

Forest Side, Ollerton. Many of the local estates built cottages for their workers and there are various clusters of such residences throughout Sherwood Forest.

Carr Brecks Farm, reminding us that much of the living in and around Sherwood Forest was based on the land.

The Forest House Guest House was situated a little way down from the Hop Pole Hotel on High Street. It is now a pub called The Snooty Fox. This advertising card has the phone number Edwinstowe 497.

Forest Road takes the traveller from Old Ollerton on to the newer part of the village based around the pit.

The New Ollerton Colliery was one of the main reasons for the development of the area called New Ollerton. This card was sent from the village just prior to the Second World War. The pit produced its first coal on 1 September 1926.

St Paulinus Church was built in 1931 of brick with a tiled roof by Greenwoods of Mansfield. The Butterley Colliery Company gave £5,000 for the building of the church while Lord Savile provided the land and £500.

New Ollerton was not entirely the result of pre-war development as this card sent in August 1909 shows. The new housing was built to the north of the old village centre.

Forest Road, New Ollerton. The writer of the card states 'this is the Main Street of our village. The shops are here and the cinema. Here we see the newsagents and "Joyce" the ladies hairdresser'. The card was posted at least thirty years after the one shown above.

SECTION FOUR
Clumber House

Clumber House was begun in 1761 by Fuller White and his work was completed by Stephen Wright around 1770. A great deal of local materials were used. Less than a century later in 1857 the 5th Duke of Newcastle had Clumber extensively changed under the architect Sir Charles Barry.

Apley Head Lodge around 1920, with a Bullnose Morris driving through. It was built in the last quarter of the eighteenth century and gave access from the Nottingham–Doncaster road along Lime Tree Avenue to the house. The grandest of the entrances, it has symmetrical lodges on either side and is surmounted by the Duke of Newcastle's arms.

The Greyhound Gates, which take their name from the statues placed on the central pillars, are one of five main entrances to Clumber Park.

Carburton Lodge has had its gates removed for many years now, but the pair of symmetrical lodges, built of ashlar under pantile roofs, remain.

Trueman's Lodge, built in 1789, gave access to the north-west corner of the park from the Worksop Road. The narrow, battlemented arch was flanked by a pair of lodges and is seen here before the First World War.

Clumber suffered a severe fire on 26 March 1879, necessitating considerable rebuilding under Charles Barry jun. This shows the west front around 1910.

Clumber House was finally demolished in 1938. After the death of the 7th Duke of Newcastle ten years earlier, his heirs had found themselves burdened by heavy taxation.

The hall contained paintings by Gainsborough, Wheatley, Hogarth and Van der Neer. The dogs seen in this painting reflect a hobby of the Dukes of Newcastle, the second of whom developed the Clumber Spaniel.

The Red Drawing Room was one of two in Clumber House. It contained many fine family portraits.

The library at Clumber was decorated in old Spanish mahogany and contained three paintings by Caxton plus first and second folios of Shakespeare.

The hallway and gallery above were built in white marble and provided an imposing entrance to the house.

Lime Tree Avenue, planted by the 4th Duke of Newcastle around 1840, covers 3 miles from Apley Head Lodge to the house and contains 1,296 trees in double rows.

Clumber Bridge, built of ashlar stone, has three semi-circular arches and dates from around 1770.

Clumber Lake was built between 1774 and 1789 at a cost of almost £7,000. Covering 83 acres, it stretches almost 2 miles commencing at the weir near Hardwick Grange.

Clumber from the bridge near the other end of the lake.

The *Lincoln*, seen here in 1906, on Clumber Lake was one of two fully rigged miniature men-of-war. It weighed 40 tons. Its companion was called the *Salamenca*.

The *Lincoln* remained on the lake until children entered the park and burnt and sank it in 1943.

The fountain in the formal gardens at Clumber. Its centre piece is said to have been carved from one solid piece of marble weighing 50 tons.

Lincoln Terrace marks the divide between the formal gardens and the lake. Incorporating marble statues and vases, much of the stone for the terrace was brought from Italy.

The Lincoln Stables were completed in the late eighteenth century using red brick under a greystone slate roof. The clock dates from 1763. After the National Trust took over Clumber Park they restored the church in 1946 and set up tea gardens to cater for the influx of visitors.

Clumber Church was built between 1886 and 1889 for the 7th Duke of Newcastle. It was designed by Bodley and Garner in the Victorian Gothic Revival style and cost £40,000.

Clumber Church, seen here around 1908, is dedicated to St Mary, has a 180 ft tower and spire and is built of white Steetley stone with red facings of Runcorn sandstone.

The Normanton Inn (pre-First World War) was situated on the Nottingham–Doncaster road adjacent to one of the entrances to Clumber Park. The building is thought originally to have been an old manor house.

The original Worksop Manor was designed by Robert Smythson and completed around 1585. It was built for the 6th Earl of Shrewsbury, who was the husband of Bess of Hardwick. The manor was destroyed by fire in October 1761.

The later Worksop Manor designed by James Paine was sold to the 4th Duke of Newcastle in 1839. Much of this was later demolished.

SECTION FIVE

Rufford Abbey

Rufford Abbey was founded by the Cistercians in the twelfth century and was run by the religious order until Henry VIII's dissolution of the monasteries in 1536, when it passed into the secular hands of the Earls of Shrewsbury. Most of the monastery was demolished over the following 140 years. A sizeable house was built around the monastical remains, with the west front shown here.

The entrance gates, erected in 1841 on the Nottingham–Doncaster road, gave access to Rufford estate which in 1938 consisted of 18,730 acres. A lime tree drive led up to the house.

Picturesque Rufford Abbey played host to many famous personages, from Edward I in 1290 to Edward VII, who attended the Rufford races up to 1908.

The west front. Rufford Abbey was inherited by the Savile family in 1626 and their descendants again rebuilt the house at the end of the seventeenth century.

In the mid-nineteenth century further substantial alterations were made to the house. This card is by R. Sneath of Paradise Street, Sheffield.

The east front of Rufford. The late Victorian years, when the estate employed 203 staff, to the 1920s with its royal visits and society balls, was a time of opulence at the abbey, but savage tax demands and the cost of running the abbey led to its sad decline.

Rufford Abbey was finally sold by the Savile family in 1938. It was nearly demolished in 1955 but is now the focal point of a country park.

The brick hall was described by Lord John Savile in 1899 thus: a 'floor of red brick in mosaic devices. A wainscot of dark oak panelling runs around the Hall and on it hangs pictures of the Tudor period . . . above the wainscot the walls are covered in tapestries of the Flemish school.'

The chapel dates from at least the sixteenth century. Its walls were covered with tapestries and the pews were carved from black oak with handsome finials.

Wellow village was established as Rufford Abbey was developed. The monks cleared their new lands causing the depopulation of the villages of Rufford, Cratley and Winkerfield, with many villagers relocating in Wellow.

SECTION SIX
Thoresby House

Thoresby House is the third substantial building to be erected on the site. The first hall, replacing an earlier mansion, was built in 1683 for the 4th Earl of Kingston, but burnt down in 1745. The second hall, designed by John Carr and commenced in 1749, was disliked by the Earls of Manvers who had it demolished.

The present Thoresby Hall was designed by Anthony Salvin in the Manorial style and built between 1864 and 1875. This view is the south side; note the scaffolding on the tower.

The west side of Thoresby Hall can be seen in this view of the hall which was built almost square. The tower in the south-west corner was deliberately designed to offset the symmetrical features of most of the hall.

Wrought-iron gates by Brown and Downing of Birmingham gave access to the east side of Thoresby where the main entrance was situated beneath the clock tower.

The east frontage was symmetrical apart from the wings, one of which was built in Scandinavian style and the other under Dutch influence. Access to the hall was through oak entrance doors.

The Robin Hood statue immediately in front of the main entrance to Thoresby Hall was designed by Tussaud-Birt, the grandson of the famous Madame Tussaud. It is a reminder that Thoresby Park was created by the enclosure of part of Sherwood Forest.

A close-up of the hall which remained in the same family, the Manvers, until after the Second World War. It was then owned for a time by British Coal; subsequently plans were made to operate it as a hotel. At the time of writing the building's future is uncertain but at least it is still standing.

The Great Hall at Thoresby was situated on the first floor and rose through three storeys to a hammer-beam roof. It was 64 ft long and 31 ft wide.

The grand staircase can be seen leaving the Great Hall at the western end giving access to balconies from which it was possible to peer down into the sumptuously furnished Great Hall below.

The library, a two-storey room, was situated on the south side of the hall. It was extravagantly equipped with books and paintings.

The carved chimney-piece above the library fireplace was the focal point of the room, showing the nearby Major Oak along with Robin Hood and Little John.

The Buck Gates, providing access to Thoresby Park, are so called because of the statues of male deer on either side of the gates.

Thoresby Bridge, situated in the park, provided a crossing point over the River Meden.

The church in Thoresby Park is contemporary to the present hall. It is dedicated to St John the Evangelist and replaced an earlier building. It is pleasantly situated opposite the estate school.

The 8th Notts T.F. Thoresby Camp, 1913, gives an example of how Thoresby was put to the national cause during the two world wars. The Second World War saw part of Thoresby being requisitioned and some of the parkland was cultivated to produce badly needed food supplies.

Welbeck Abbey

The original Welbeck Abbey was founded in the reign of King Stephen. At the dissolution it passed eventually to the Cavendish family who became the Dukes of Newcastle. In the eighteenth century it came by marriage into the hands of the Dukes of Portland.

The Lion Gates were constructed for the 6th Duke of Portland in 1894. The gate piers each have a lion on top holding a shield bearing the family crest. The large gates were mechanically operated from the adjacent lodge.

A Welbeck lodge of which there were between forty and fifty by 1880. Most were of similar design and built of local Steetley stone.

Welbeck was developed as a private residence in the sixteenth and early seventeenth centuries, and both James I and Charles I stayed there. Further alterations took place in the eighteenth century.

Entrance to Welbeck Abbey. It was the 5th Duke of Portland who carried out most of the alterations to Welbeck between 1854 and 1879.

Welbeck Abbey Chapel and kitchen wing. In the 1950s much of Welbeck Abbey was leased to the Army to become Welbeck College. Today the college authorities jealously retain their privacy.

The Oxford wing was largely destroyed by fire on 5 October 1900. It was rebuilt to designs by Sir Ernest George.

The lake was designed by Humphrey Repton in 1789 and was later extended to 3 miles in length by the 5th Duke of Portland.

The impressive entrance hall to Welbeck contained fine pieces of Flemish tapestry based on illustrations from the 1st duke's book on horsemanship.

The billiard room was one of many rooms in the abbey. It was decorated with a number of sporting prints, especially of racehorses.

The swan drawing-room took its name from the swan depicted on the Axminster carpet.

The state drawing-room's walls were hung with French tapestries. Above, the cornices were enriched with white and gold.

The Gothic hall was remodelled in the Gothic style by the Countess of Oxford around 1734. Her coat of arms can be seen over the fireplace. Sir Ernest George supervised other alterations after the fire in 1900.

The chapel was in part of the old riding school and was opened in December 1892.

The staircase to the Titchfield Library was converted from part of the old riding school in the 1890s.

The Titchfield Library was separated from the chapel by an organ gallery which can be seen here at the end of the room.

The print corridor was over 200 ft in length and joined the old riding school to the main part of the abbey.

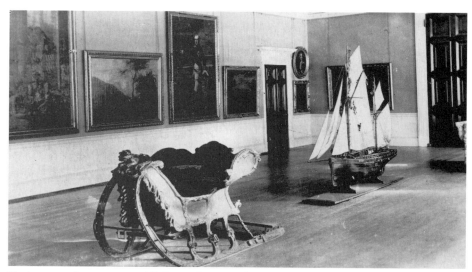

Underground ante-room. All the underground rooms were painted in plain salmon pink with white ceilings. Various collections of paintings, models and stuffed birds were housed here in surprisingly mild conditions.

The underground ballroom was 159 ft 2 in long and 63 ft 7 in wide. It was called the underground picture gallery and was lit by eighteen chandeliers and twenty-seven octagonal skylights.

The underground ballroom was able to cater for 1,200 guests when the King and Queen of Spain paid a visit to Welbeck.

The entrance to the short tunnel. The eccentric 5th duke was nicknamed the 'Burrowing Duke' and instigated extensive underground building, employing upwards of 1,500 men.

The entrance to the long tunnel. The 5th duke, who valued his privacy, was eventually able to drive by carriage through tunnels from the abbey to the edge of his estate.

The Dukes Archway was built by the 5th duke at Clipstone and was modelled on Worksop's fourteenth-century gateway. It was part of the duke's plan for a 21 mile avenue of trees from Welbeck to Nottingham.

The Winnings were built by the 6th duke in 1890, providing six homes for aged ex-servants. The name comes from the fact that the duke financed them from four racehorse winners in the Classics of 1888–90.

Offices and stables. The latter contained stalls for ninety-six horses.

The riding school was built of local stone and was 379 ft long, 106 ft wide and 50 ft high.

Inside the riding school were cast-iron columns on each side, at the top of which were gas jets to provide lighting.

The school, Welbeck, served the families of the estate workers. The sender of this card in 1908 says, 'I am sending in my application for these schools. The result is very doubtful as they are quite satisfied with the head they have.'

The post office was another amenity for the estate, built for the 5th duke by C. & A. Dennett. Local stone was used and it was finished around 1861.

The laundry was completed at the same time as the post office and by the same company.

The fruit arcade was only part of a series of fruit hot houses. It extended over 700 ft in length with ornamented iron arches and contained apple, pear and peach trees. Grapes, pineapples and strawberries were also grown at Welbeck.

The ornamental well – one of the features in the Welbeck gardens.

The fountain and tea house. Although the 5th duke was somewhat reclusive he instigated various outdoor building works but these were often only enjoyed by visitors and the servants.

Welbeck Camp. Parts of the estate were given over to the military during the First World War. A hospital for wounded soldiers operated from Welbeck.

The temple was one of a number of small buildings found in Welbeck Abbey's grounds.

The cricket ground and pavilion were only some of the amenities on the estate. An eighteen-hole golf course also existed until it was damaged by troops stationed there during the Second World War.

The 6th Duke of Portland was a distant cousin of the 5th duke who died in December 1879 leaving no offspring. The photograph shows him replying to deputations at his silver wedding celebrations in June 1914.

The 6th Duke of Portland, William John Arthur Charles James Cavendish Bentinck, married Winifred Dallas Yorke in 1889. The photograph shows their silver wedding celebrations.

Festivities for the silver wedding anniversary took place over three days in June 1914 and involved 26,000 local children.

SECTION EIGHT

Around and About

Worksop station, prior to the First World War. After reaching the edge of Welbeck estate via an underground tunnel the secretive 5th Duke of Portland would travel in a closed carriage to Worksop station where the carriage and its occupants would entrain for London, still unseen by the general public.

Ye Old Ship, Worksop, towards the end of the nineteenth century. Many Worksop inns formed the Dukeries Posting Proprietor's Association to organize horse-drawn carriage trips round the Dukeries and Sherwood Forest.

The George was one of Worksop's most historic inns. The privileged carriages had keys to enter the private Dukeries parks on Tuesdays, Thursdays and Saturdays.

Cuckney, a picturesque forest village which has always been of importance because of its mills.

Many of the Welbeck estate workers lived in Cuckney. Its church is Norman in origin.

Carburton Church today serves a minute forest settlement.

The Carburton fountain situated by an attractive stretch of water. In earlier times Carburton was a flourishing forest village.

St Peter's Church, Mansfield. Mansfield is known as 'The Old Forest Town of Mansfield'.

The Centre Tree situated in West Gate, Mansfield, was said to mark the centre of the ancient Sherwood Forest. It was demolished by a lorry in the black-out in 1935.

The Bentinck Monument standing in Mansfield market place is to Lord George
Bentinck, the son of the 4th Duke of Portland who died in 1848 while walking from
Welbeck Abbey to Thoresby Hall.

Wellow is a forest village traditionally built around a village green with its maypole. Flanking the green can be seen places of both sin (The Red Lion, right, and The Durham Ox, centre) and redemption (the chapel, left). A maypole remains today although it is a modern construction, replacing the one seen in the photograph.

Laxton, to the eastern edge of Sherwood Forest, is unique in England, being the only village where the three open-field system of farming continues to this day, administered by a manorial court. In medieval times Laxton, being on high ground (220 ft above sea level) was chosen as a site for a motte and bailey castle, which looked out on the royal forest of Sherwood and played host to royalty from Henry II to Edward I.

The Forest Folk, Blidworth, opened in 1926 and took its name from the novel by James Prior Kirk. The hotel was decorated with stained-glass windows depicting scenes from the book, which was set in Sherwood Forest.

Blidworth features in the Robin Hood legend; Will Scarlet and Maid Marian are said to have lived here.

Blidworth Church has a monument inside to Thomas Leake, a sixteenth-century forest ranger who is said to have died in Sherwood Forest.

Main Street, Calverton, in the 1920s. Along with Linby, Mansfield and Edwinstowe, Calverton was the site of one of the six-weekly Swainmotes or Verderer Courts when petty offences committed in the forest were dealt with.

Main Street, Calverton. In 1589 the village rector Revd William Lee invented the stocking frame here.

Woodborough village close to Calverton has a medieval church. The adjacent twentieth-century mock-Tudor style inn takes its name from the number of bells in the church tower.

Woodborough, like Calverton, had many framework knitters' cottages.

Newstead Abbey, the family home of the poet Byron, is situated in what was part of Sherwood Forest.

Newstead Abbey is close to the spot known as Fountaindale where it is said Friar Tuck once lived.

Top cross, Linby. Many claim that Linby, with its stone buildings, is the most attractive of the Sherwood Forest villages.

Bottom cross, Linby. The village is unusual in having two crosses; some maintain that the crosses were formerly boundary markers for the forest.

Papplewick, between Newstead and Linby, is by legend supposed to be the place where Robin Hood stabled his horses in a cavity in some rocks before venturing into Nottingham on foot.

Papplewick Church is said to be where a member of Robin Hood's band of outlaws, Alan a'Dale, was married. This church was built in 1793.

Bestwood is important as it is the most southerly surviving part of the old Sherwood Forest. The park was originally enclosed in 1650.

Charles II gave Bestwood to his illegitimate son by Nell Gwyn whom he made 1st Duke of St Albans. The 10th duke built the present lodge in the 1860s.

A sixteenth-century impression of Nottingham Castle. Nottingham was the southern gateway to the forest with many early monarchs using the castle as a base for hunting in the forest.

Robin Hood's statue outside Nottingham Castle. The legend of Robin Hood has the Sheriff of Nottingham, based in the castle, as Robin's chief enemy.

Nottingham Castle today is a nineteenth-century mansion house, with none of the medieval feel of Robin Hood's time.

Ye Olde Trip to Jerusalem, nestling close up to the rocks of Nottingham Castle, is said to date from 1189. Soldiers on the way to the crusades are claimed to have stayed there.

Hurrah For The Sherwood Foresters!

Bravo, brave Sherwood Foresters!
In many a desperate fray
You've tackled the foe and laid him low
In the good old British way!
Though Home be far, fond loving hearts
Are with you in battle stern;
So here's the best of luck, brave lads
Till in triumph you return.

The Sherwood Foresters took their name from the local forest.

The Sherwood Foresters was the nickname of the territorial battalion of the Notts and Derby Regiment.

VIVIT POST FUNERA VIRTUS

CITY OF NOTTINGHAM

Robin Hood's link with Nottingham is known worldwide. The Goss China Company incorporated the Nottingham crest onto this drinking cup.

Acknowledgements

Thanks are due to the staffs of various local libraries for their patient help and advice. Also grateful thanks to the numerous people in the postcard world who supplied the cards.

Attempts have been made to contact all copyright holders to obtain permission to use their work. If any have been unintentionally missed out I apologize.